Twice Told

AKRON SERIES IN POETRY

AKRON SERIES IN POETRY
Mary Biddinger, Editor

Caryl Pagel, *Twice Told*
Emily Rosko, *Weather Inventions*
Emilia Phillips, *Empty Clip*
Anne Barngrover, *Brazen Creature*
Matthew Guenette, *Vasectomania*
Sandra Simonds, *Further Problems with Pleasure*
Leslie Harrison, *The Book of Endings*
Emilia Phillips, *Groundspeed*
Philip Metres, *Pictures at an Exhibition: A Petersburg Album*
Jennifer Moore, *The Veronica Maneuver*
Brittany Cavallaro, *Girl-King*
Oliver de la Paz, *Post Subject: A Fable*
John Repp, *Fat Jersey Blues*
Emilia Phillips, *Signaletics*
Seth Abramson, *Thievery*
Steve Kistulentz, *Little Black Daydream*
Jason Bredle, *Carnival*
Emily Rosko, *Prop Rockery*
Alison Pelegrin, *Hurricane Party*
Matthew Guenette, *American Busboy*
Joshua Harmon, *Le Spleen de Poughkeepsie*

Titles published since 2010.
For a complete listing of titles published in the series,
go to www.uakron.edu/uapress/poetry.

Twice Told

Caryl Pagel

The University of Akron Press
Akron, Ohio

• First Edition 2019 • Manufactured in the United States of America.
All inquiries and permission requests should be addressed to the publisher,
The University of Akron Press, Akron, Ohio 44325-1703.

ISBN: 978-1-629221-69-4 (paper)
ISBN: 978-1-629221-70-0 (ePDF)
ISBN: 978-1-629221-71-7 (ePub)

A catalog record for this title is available from the Library of Congress.

∞The paper used in this publication meets the minimum requirements of ANSI/NISO z39.48–1992 (Permanence of Paper).

Cover image: Heidi Reszies
Cover design: Amy Freels

Twice Told was designed and typeset in Bembo, with Futura display, by Amy Freels and printed on sixty-pound natural and bound by Bookmasters of Ashland, Ohio.

Contents

You are my other country
and I find it hard going
—Lorine Niedecker

Old Wars

You are trying to remember how
it happened You are trying to
remember these events in a sensible
order The narrator you think met
the old woman on a train
She had been to war or
at least you think you recall
reading that she said she had
The story started on the train
The narrator in this case was
mostly incidental The narrator in this
case was made to listen patiently
and account for The woman's tale
you recall was too strange to
be told straight You needed to
hear it from a distance From
another mouth or source The narrator
met the woman on a train
She had been to war The
story was about the woman and
her experiences at war or more
precisely *in it* as a victim
and a corpse and someone who
was marched straight to and through
the brink of death—who gazed
deep into death's vile and wintry
irises—before saving the crowd of
innocent people she had been marching

with   They were on the side
of the road   You remember this
detail   They were on a dusty
black road being marched to death
and you know this because the
narrator is delivering this information within
a story via another story—a
story told by the same old
woman who may or may not
have existed whom he may or
may not have met on a
train who may or may not
but most likely was a part
of the war   She was not
a hero   She must have been
a hero you think for having
protected all of those people for
sacrificing her own soul her own
hands her own fragile sense of
self and yet there are no
heroes here   Not the patient
narrator   Not you for trying to
remember   Not even the woman who
told the story for war knows
no heroes and makes a fool
of every witness which—right now—
through memory—is both you and
this incidental narrator and whomever you
are telling the story to   You
are trying to remember how it
happened   There was a woman on
a train   This woman told a
story not to you but you

read the story that she told
from the narrator's point of view
and now you know it   How
she abandoned her own consciousness to
swap bodies with the officer   She
parted with her own old heart
She left her mind behind   She
became a monster and master and
through this brave and magical transformation
was able to save a small
population of souls or so she
said that day to the one
you know as her train mate

Telephone

There was fear involved—yes—some
fear and hesitancy to discuss what
you knew you had done but
had not yet told anyone   It
was nothing   You discussed it for
hours—all that nothing and what
nothing meant—what a shame it
would be to allow the nothing
to decay—to fade and fly
and die like all those nothings
that you both had had before
It felt like a new nothing
but you knew—instinctually—in your
frantic animal soul—that all nothing
sustains itself the same way—by
expanding—cracking—swallowing itself and all
around it—by colliding with old
nothings   You knew and discussed what
a nothing all your nothing was—
and yet you could not find
an end to it   This kind of
nothing kept going   It kept going
into itself and back out again
around the day—winding itself through
you and whispering things concerning you
across the wire and in sleep's
abysmal strangle and after all that
talk you felt true   Like a
new version of yourself you never

knew   A version of the very
dreadful nothing that you had always
had a vision of yourself becoming

The Traveler

The only fact to continue to
bear is suffering and the suffering
itself is what one requires to
exist—it is purely grief that
prevents one from vanishing completely   And
care   You read that she knew
the facts firsthand because she saw
them happen   She met the traveler—
a total stranger—who was passing
through their town in the midst of
an intricate blizzard when he first
spotted and asked everyone about the
two of them—everyone in town
about the strange lanky man seen
rambling down the main street with
such a severely pained look staining
his strained face that one could
never forget it   The events occurred
some years before one source confirmed
The man had had a sickly
wife—still did—and his life
was cloaked with a harsh ache
The tale progressed accordingly   By the
end of the story—which was
complete with drama and deception and
hunger and grief—with shadows and
sobs and flurries—with fraught evenings
made quiet by the most intimate
glances and gestures—the man had

fallen in lust and love and
right back out and through them
It was a distressing story after
all   Poignant and moving and true
you knew but not without its
sorrows   The traveler who initially solicited
the story's performance must have thought
the same things—you could sympathize
with his interest in rumor and
hearsay   You wondered if he appeared
at all improved having listened to
the twisted and terrific details that
still haunt a total stranger's drab
past   You are feeling for once
transformed by the narrative and will
not be asked to mask it

Rumors

You are telling the story   You
are telling the story again   Twice
told you tell him the story
someone he knows told you   You
know the same someone the same
story but different aspects and facets
You were not present in this
story but in one story he
was and it was told to
you by someone you both know
You tell him another story about
himself that even he didn't know—
but you knew   You've known about
his story for quite some time
without knowing him and he knows
you   He recalls when you first
told a story—not the one
you are telling right now but
still true   You keep telling   You
want to keep telling him and
so you do and he does
too and at first you are
standing in the same place not
telling the story—just clues—because
you knew that you were going
to tell this story and it alarms
you that you knew   Your
sudden sentence is closing the room
He is telling a story that

is oddly similar to the story
told by you   It might be
a part of the same story—
a larger story—larger than you
or your telling of the story
or his telling it back to
you anew   But by now there
is just one story with two
tellers and it endures through both
the telling and the endless loop
that continues with or without you

Four Dead Men

He took a solitary walk across
the region He couldn't stop he
couldn't stop he couldn't pause he
couldn't stop he sought to circle
the space He needed to circle
the space you see He needed
to see the place you see
he could only fathom the place
he knew you see if he
saw it plainly as he circled
and you heard that he recorded
his thoughts on the walk at
the hospital His walk began—so
the story goes—as *the dog*
days were drawing to an end
It was the finish of one
mood and the commencement of another
He was going to conclude unmoving
he knew you see he would
eventually break down immobile you know
only realizing in retrospect—after the
act of walking—but before recording—
that he could remember the faces
he encountered if he began to
watch once more—if he took
a walk around the region in
his mind—if he recalled the
damage that he'd done and wrote
it down At that time this

man—this first dead man—was
attempting to make things appear you
see he was attempting to reclaim
that which in his mind had
wholly vanished He was feeling—in
fact—a little apparitional He was
attempting to think himself healthy you
know he wanted to walk himself
well and so he wrote down
what he saw and you experienced
what he saw within the stretched
and spooky spiraling sentences that unraveled
and expanded as a rough path
parallels a road that no one
is headed down They wouldn't stop
He couldn't stop He disclosed you
know in prose the destruction of
important historical buildings He witnessed the
wreck of ancient languages He saw
old ruins which recalled him to
new ruins some of which he
was seeing again in his mind
and some of which he read
about and some of which you
were reading about him reading about
and some of which he knew
from the very few people he
had stopped long enough to talk
to This man—this first dead
man—admired the wildest gardens you
know but he also couldn't stop
picturing his passed friends' faces he
wrote he couldn't stop thinking dead

strangers' thoughts you read he couldn't
stop He couldn't stop He couldn't
stop and didn't want to You
are shocked now abruptly up from
a page on which he is
describing the interesting history of herring
to see another man hovering—*here*—
in your doorway This other man—
this second man is living and
you love him but he can't stop
he can't see—you can't stop
he can't see he needs someone
to take him to the hospital
He needs someone to circle his
sickness He needs you and only
you to circle his circles and
you're not—you're going to stop
You read instead a book about
a man who has recently been
in the hospital This man is
leaving in part to see the
now empty home of a friend
who had recently passed in part
perhaps because he should have remained
in the hospital Instead this man—
this third man dead—is visiting
his friend's home just after he
died—a suicide—with the hope
that he—the third dead man—
could inhabit again the tone and
humor and luminous brilliant beautiful significant
wonderful loving tortured sorrowful stagnant angry
awesome puzzled tragic hurtful magic difficult

mind of his dear friend during
the time in which he still
survived—when this man was not
yet ill but lived instead to
write about architecture and remarkable buildings

Ghost Towns

There is not a name for
how you felt in the meantime
There is not a name for
what you would most like to
hide   How are you supposed to
explain it if there is no
name   A name is what you
need to become a little less
invisible   A name is what you
need to die   But what if
you have no stake in this
decrepit town   No title or claim
to your one own only cause

The Motley Cow

She told you at dinner although
she had told this story before
It was a story of madness
and rage—of compassion and faith
and the reaches of her grief
after her dear father died   You
did not interrupt her to discuss
your own grief   Your own terrible
grief after the death of your own
dear father because this was in fact
her story and she was telling
it—and it was dinner   She
had told this story before   You
noticed that the third person at
the table had already heard this
story—and therefore could help her
tell it   The third person could
remember some of the details for
her friend and alleviate the stress
of having to tell this story—again—
alone—to you—although it was
a meaningful story and one she
wished to tell again at dinner
In the telling of this tragic
tale—a tale concerning misplaced affection—
intrigue and hate and the awful
stages of old age where a
man might become a monster not
only to his own wife but

also to improper objects of affection—
in this telling some of the
anger and pain split away and
was replaced by pleasure   In this
particular circumstance the teller had come
a long way that very day
from a place she no longer
loved—the place of the story—
to *this* place and *this* dinner
and *this* flicker and *this* fade
of *these* shadows thrown by *those*
candles as patrons settled payment and
absented themselves through the exact exit
that brought them into and through
the location of her story told

The Badlands

You note there is a hole
for where the heart once was
and a horizon for where the
eye was once and an absence
for where the animals—once—were
watching   The bloody buffalo body—once
tender and upright—was pierced you
heard through the heart that is
now the hole in the growing
hollow of a grey frame   Your
friend the painter claimed that this
was the wild west and in
the wild west there is nothing
else to be gained but further
destruction   Your friend the painter paints
something that is not a bleeding
and something that is not meaning
but instead reveals the vision of
a version of the story that
you couldn't believe had actually emerged
yet   Imagine a massive animal body
slow and wait   It freaks and
breaks   Imagine the animal body dropped
in death amidst great waves of
winter plains—stained by bitter crimson
notes in an unknown language   Imagine
the figure—implied by the hole—that
in this particular case records the
presence of the prey that never
ambled   Recall that at first there

was no legend   So you started
with fauna   You started with the
hunt and knew that if he
could paint the lack of animals
than you could pen LAST—and
BUFFALO—and HEART—and it would
happen   You could write of frantic
paths stamped through the badlands and
radical lady sharpshooters and robbers rampant
on the lam and flowers   You
could write of the tallgrass   You
could write of the green   You
could write of the roiling sea
some settlers saw in the rolling wheat
while walking—famished and desperate—toward
far coasts and freedom   You could
mention horizons that signaled flight or
the brittle Midwest landscape that swallowed
families whole—or the circus of
tired humans that—once upon a
time—one could pay to watch
paraded through a small town   You
could write of how everything that
dies is eventually archived   Of railroads
and radios and posts and the
single survivor whom you both had
decided in her brash and somber
splendor captured the very last buffalo
heart in all the land to
make a bare and daring gift
of it to her sullen lover and—
once disregarded—this action marked the
end of the wild west and
the beginning of our tame days

Supposed To

You are not supposed to know things before they happen

You are not supposed to tell the story before it has had time to occur

The way you feel feels like a sideways yanking vertigo insisting your
present tranquil self straight through your future splitting self and
viewing that future self sputtering tendrils of lapsed instants back at
your concrete and passing calamitous absence

It is a speeding up or a quickening heartsick

Like the reverie before breaking asleep you seek to race way out ahead
of the turn in order to squint back at what has yet to ensue

You are not supposed to know

You did not ask to know

You do not desire to lose the control implicit in what's random or the
absolute and manageable assurance of reasonable and reliable
happenstance

Mausoleum

The night behaved exactly as you
thought it would As you saw
it would As you saw it
unfold and unravel and pre-occur in
a previously—you now know—prescient
premonition The details are irrelevant You
saw the night tumble forth anxiously
with rare nerves as if swerving
away from a ghost train Perhaps
it was almost dusk There was
or maybe there could have been
a dreadful storm But there was
no storm You had the feeling
that it was later than it
really was Maybe it was a
different day or if the same
day than you saw this day
tilt and stretch and sway and
strain itself against the previously—aforementioned—
vision—as—to be honest—at
this point—you knew it would
The version of the night you
saw occurred as a sudden shot
straight through the actual night that
was just about to start occurring
The night tried to hold itself
upright—tried to be true to
its given name—to remain faithful
and patient—such a great trait—

through sorrow and flawed stakes—through
the terrible rest of dreamers each
reading their own imperceptible story
You were worried   The precise details
are irrelevant   The events of the
night occurred as observed   Not set forth
by you but seen into and
through—planned perhaps by the unseen
forces that occasionally reveal an intricate
narrative briefly perceivable   It was the
next day   Or that same day
Or a different night that you
found yourself taking a quick picture
of the man as he stood
patiently waiting beneath his own engraved
name in the blazing rays of
the graveyard   That name—his same
name—was presently labeling a mausoleum
No strangers were present   Or if
they were you couldn't sense them
There was no proof   That night
and then again that same day
you knew that when he looked
at you you would shift your
gaze away   That when he looked
at you you would hide   Perhaps
it was night   Perhaps a different
day   You knew you would veil
your startled stare so that he
could not grasp or catch your
very instant vision of his death
in the black and brittle—damp
and bewildered—echo of your loud

eyes Because as you found then—
and as you note now—there
is never any proof There is
never any sufficient evidence So—to
you—there is also no truer
tender kindness than disguise But recognize—
one can always find that loving
feeling by returning to the mausoleum

Interior & Wall

Vision #1

Was it a coincidence you wondered standing there or was
it some sort of fate occurring by the desire of your own mind as it
willed V to appear in a borrowed car on the corner of Dodge and
Jefferson you willed
a friend to appear because you were out for a
walk with nowhere to go and you couldn't stay home so you walked
toward and around the town until you felt the vehicle drawn toward
the precise place that you walked and also sensed all at once that you
were the
one it was headed to and in just one
second you would open a dark maroon and silver door and in one
more second
you would climb into the car and V would say he would drive you
with him in the direction of the other cars with
which the traffic of the day kept up he said which
way and you felt you were meant to be silent so it didn't much matter
just any way

Vision #2

You knew those two were together you
were folding laundry at M's you were
doing nothing important you were doing
and thinking nothing important when you imagined those two and
their words as catastrophic underground echoes their
bodies occupying the same place you cannot explain it your body
in a far off place existing removed in
a very separate space you were folding laundry when you experienced a
vision the vision
came rapidly through you it came
to you from nowhere you thought to
tell someone you found a phone and picked it up but didn't use it you
  couldn't tell
anyone because anyone
in their right mind would wonder if in
fact you were unable anymore to discern the facts
from magic or an active imagination from
some false sense of acquaintance or some
happenstance you recall it was a Sunday you were at M's house nothing
  was happening
and it was summer where you were but you felt a chill and
knew the two of them were together somewhere those two whom you
  once knew

Vision #3

What could happen next is what
you are concerned with knowing you
are not alone in this there are
whole days gone off to dirt and matter refracting whole
minutes and weeks wasted wondering which modest obstinate minute
might transform this gesture into uproar cough into loss or might
move the route to work or door forever and once moved
what interior transformation what
could happen next what could
be imagined before ever once occurring or could it be
made simply by saying it you know you made
this day in mind before it happened it wasn't originally intended to be
like this

Vision #4

You see families in loud matching outfits you
see the face next door is performing a series of peculiar signals you see
it began right here in mud and shale it
arrived out of nowhere right here this town you are currently residing
  in arrived
in the dark it arrived in
the center of an arid lowland you read in some forgotten source that
  for the
homesteaders . . . the harshest of hardships was loneliness and for the
  homesteaders
there was no mention of ending there
was no mention of continuing there was
a constant crawling motion as they built dwellings in dwindling
  moonlight and D said a
lot you couldn't respond to that night you stood in the parking lot
there was a streetlight reflecting his gestures you saw it all happen
  again right over there

Vision #5

One kind of absolute actual ceaseless love is the one
where you are trying to keep your beloved alive where
ever he goes you are trying not to let him ever
die one type of enduring true love is a constant anxious vigilance
  one way to die
is love is
not allowing death you will not
but who sees you you want to know this plan of course has flaws but
you cannot let it you
cannot assent to or collapse in the path of another's ever evolving
  vanishing you cannot
watch this kind of pain and yet what is another option that you
  won't watch

Vision #6

You met the fiancés at the bar you
saw two months had passed you saw
but did not know who played your favorite song and something was
  gone you knew but
what what
was it that was gone it was
already better without it it was already
a part of your fractured past a
portion of the future's forgetting or perhaps a portion
of something you had never known you talked about plans and
  travel of
their upcoming excursion to France and of their
recent move to New York and of your recent
decision to see Amsterdam and of their upcoming decision
to join you in a place that wasn't this place and to
tell a joke that was this joke but to tell
it in a way that recreated the very night that you were in and to keep it
to experience again this joy you were already then a part of and having
  but wanting too

Vision #7

So much that summer was occurring on the sidewalk in front of
  George's so
much you almost forgot how much
had also taken place on and in front of the upright pianos that the
  town you were in had
scattered around haphazardly they were scattered
everywhere on the sidewalk and everywhere
you went like now on Linn and Market how this music heats
  internally to extend you

Vision #8

That sunken unlit house that
was crammed with screaming souls was
there before you swear but now it wasn't or was it you wonder as you stare was there
anything there before anything
that should have been a clue you knew perhaps you knew you should have known that

Vision #9

Another kind of love is not existent it is insisted you cannot declare it
aloud another
kind is where you are so nothing you cannot presume a kindness
or a consequence you cannot imagine action or
look for anything more meaningfully material than the mundane look
of the immediate you have committed to not leaning into a part of
a something but a
nothing in this case is what you are and what you will remain because
a nothing
is safe inside itself an absence is not disclosed it stays the apparition that
it always is

Vision #10

Assume Z's premonition a few days before the event made it real
assume
that all the threading vigor was creating other matter that
each of these small actions works to hinge each
other together a woman outside your window is speaking through her
child another
perfect dusk it is an absolutely eternally perfect
evening you note from the balcony as you perceive the wave in motion
this evening
while you sleep and hear an ocean crash to shore it's traffic and you are
moved awhile

The Heart

The heart just won't stop   You
try and you try   You yank
up plies and push it down
deep under the floorboards   It won't
stay   It won't stop   That's not
quite the right account but you
are attempting to re-state the plot
In this case the floor becomes
a door into a muddled memory
of a gory story and twice
now you've confused the scene of
a hacked up corpse with the
end of another horrifying chronicle which—
of course—couldn't have happened exactly
the way you explained it and—
in fact—might even have occurred
in your own life   Now observe
how despite a lack of accurate
facts you will still permit yourself
to speak—for to tell a
story poorly is an ancient disease
The woman described the instant in
which she heard a recording cry
out from the mouth of a
headstone   There was just one button—
imitating death's tone   The device belonged
to one already gone and he
was long in professing his affection
for his once still grieving breathing

love   His living other   Though—the
woman said—she noticed the bride's
name buried far from the persistence
of her groom's unrelenting passing   His
strange strained refrain   The story of
the heart is that it just
won't stop   It talks and talks

Home

He asked you to make sure
that she got home in time—
then he asked you to confirm
that she had a ride He
knew several things you couldn't know—
like when it was she should
be going home You knew too
a few things that he did
not In this case it was
that the time it was right
then was not the time "Time"
said it was It was not
the time he thought it was
The time it was right then
was neither the time he thought
nor the time you really knew
it to be but you could
not tell him this She needs
a ride home he said She
needs a ride home in time
He asked you if you would
watch out for her Could you
make sure that she gets home
You said you would make sure
that she would get home in
time You understood—though—that you
could not actually make sure that
she got home because there was
no time and so there was

no home and if there was
either a home or time or
a "home-in-time" then that
was exactly where she already was—
as were you   You both were
right here where he was and
also where it was that he
wanted you two to be   He
was in his own home but
he was also in his mind's
time—and in this mind's time
she was not yet his wife
and you were not yet his
daughter—because—in this time—his
mind's time—he was a long
time ago and just attempting to
get your mother home   He was
requesting your help and you lied
He was asking you to promise
her promptness   He wanted you to
ensure that she always and forever
arrived safely wherever it was that
she was going because in the
time of his mind right then there
was a curfew and he needed
to get her home in time

A Little Apparitional

Sideways into death you go—
you're sorry so
you don't look

Museum

The soldier's wife you read hadn't
owned a photo of her lover
while he was alive   The plaque
described how after his violent and
untimely death the family was forced
to mourn the image of another
man—one whose face they were
assured was a close enough approximation

Into The Woods

A beautiful animal body lie alone
in the moonlit clearing   This animal
body was a body that had
exhausted its life feeding other animal
bodies with concern and sturdy work
and a stubborn sense of duty
as well as an acquaintance with
the worth of hunger and happenstance
and the situation that this body
had willingly or not become a
dependable part of   The brothers knew
no—*how could they know?*—part
of this when they were confronted
with the body of this beauty
one night shortly after they had
ditched their paper route in order
to follow a few hunters into
the woods after not quite a
hunch—really—but hearsay   The brothers
could not be sure of what
they saw   Some would say it
was a simple matter   Some would
say a dead animal body—a
beautiful animal body dead—is the
most simple matter there is and
beg only for further facts and
a story—but these young boys—
these brothers—had not yet in
their lives witnessed either death or

the body of a woman nude
no longer breathing   It was the
heart of winter and they were
freezing   What kinds of dogs were
these   What kinds of trees and
where did this human come from
You want to know these things
but cannot ask the brothers
because the brothers have been invented—
although—to be fair—the younger
of the two is candid and
perceptive and he was the one
who honestly illustrated the story—at
least to you   In the story
that they were existing in the
elder brother told the tale to
both his mother and sister but
the younger brother was the one
to whom the story stuck and
even after many years this brother
couldn't shake the sensation that the
details were not initially expressed right
Or not *not right* exactly but
that there was something more that
had happened that night than either
could ever tell about   One could
not tell the woman's final sighting
One could not even really imagine
what it was she thought that
winter evening as she slumped against
a trunk in the woods inhaling the
icy sharp portions of her last
gasps   One could never know—the

brother knew—the compassion that
the dogs had had for another
animal's flailing body—or the razed
dread that kept them distant but
looping and oddly ceremonial—or the
internal mechanisms of woods at dusk
that do cocoon a body safely
either until daylight or the glow
that comes from the eyes of
searchers One could never know
how in the end an old
woman could become young again and
stunning One could not know why
her meat did not feed the
other—dancing—dogs when her primary
purpose in life had been to
nourish leaching beasts But one could
intuit and inhabit this uncertainty—one
could possess it—and more importantly—
according to the younger brother—one
could recall this particular instance and
consider it on the cusp of
one's own demise—although in this
scenario—years later—our hero survived
and the story of her death
in fact might have been what
it was that ultimately saved him

Construction of a Coffin

He held up
the board the
board knotted For
his mother he
held up the
board its knots
heralded reply He
re-plied the board
He re-pried he
Knots small as
her eyes mother's
eyes set firm
in *No* He
held the board
high the board
knotted Held up
the board he
held up Held
up the board
She saw nodded
From the field
we came up
and upon them
We saw him
raise high the
boards Saw her
prodding We walked
through the house
out the back

We saw her
nod We heard
his saw and
when we heard
his saw we
all lay down

The Haunting

There is always another wife you
learn there is always a second
set of events that precedes this
one   There is always another love—
a mistress—governess—or charming young
maiden passing through town in the
service of an affluent auntie or
patron   She is often of modest
means of course but laughs like
a faultless angel   There is always
another woman   She is sometimes kept—
you learn—in the attic and
sometimes dead—*how tragic*—but always
her absent body is what gave
birth to the strange unstated and
straining exchanges that sentence your new
life   Once when you were young
you committed errors   Once when you
were young you fell in love
with a moody bard   There were
no stakes and from the grave
in which you wait you have
little to do but forever regret
it   There is always more prelude
than tale   There is always the
buried mark of the gaze that
came before the one you gave
him   You should have heeded their
warnings   You should have attended better

to the morals of their stories
Here you pause atop the spiral
staircase—hesitating before descending   You have
donned his first wife's ball gown
You feel where she fit   Since
you had the chance to choose
this route you assume you're ruined

Scenic, SD

Gathered: inexplicably concurrent gestures.
Felt: fearful of death foretold.

Seen: sign announcing the sale of Scenic.
Desired: sky on the sly.

Penned: *vacant land, surprised eyes.*
Shared: the term for severely eroded landscapes.

Wounded: the brains of that poor grilled aviator.
Wondered: what endures the Western moon?

Read: pendulums, tombs, railroads, ruins.
Understood: everyone missed disappearing.

"Here, drink this healing water," she said.
"The population is nine."

Asked: hazardous hypothetical questions.
Experienced: an endless stone road to Crescent.

Suspected: the terror of a new way of behaving.
Predicted: the terror of this way taking over.

The great woman writer of ghost stories, she told him, was eclipsed by the great man writer of ghost stories.
"Get out of the car," he ordered, "and look at this wildlife refuge."

In hindsight, the sepia photograph of the town is what made the town
handsome.
Loved: the car that harbored them.

Retained: an alarm for the unharmed.
Developed: a dread for the undead.

Rumored: to be happy is to ignore everything or nothing all at once.
It was not immediately regrettable.

Young Man Afraid of His Horses

What will keep you from telling it to everyone

What will prevent you from perpetual disclosure: shame or privacy—
words or the sense that once said you cannot snatch the story back

What you say will disseminate and break

It will split out into the ether outlasting matter—ignoring teller—
resisting order—beyond reason—escaping even your own hold on the
subject

It will not fit into history

You cannot keep yourself from speaking

Olde Main Street Inn

He was chained to the tree
and then burned to death Chained
in the woods and then lit
on fire The experts she told
you one morning in Chadron Nebraska
as he finished his juice—*grapefruit*—
were satisfied The locals were calling
it suicide You remember her saying
that detectives had considered the case
for months and many were abandoning
homicide Perched on the edge of
a barstool she explained to you
both that the man had been
teaching at a nearby college She
said he had been a teacher
at the nearby college—maybe—you
wondered later—because she already knew
you were too She could see
that you were into her story
She was an expert at recalling
this story She was pleasant and
kind and from Chadron She had
spent most of her life here
in Chadron She knew more than
you would ever know—even if
you started now—about Chadron and
the people of Chadron You knew
more than she would ever know
about absolutely nothing The man from

the story knew more than either
you or the woman telling you
about him would ever know about
being chained to a tree and
then burned to death—attached to
a pyre and then lit on
fire   You wish to accurately relate
her version   You wish to faithfully
relate her version   You wish to
relate her version and the vision
of those events as she conveyed
them to you both on that
dusty summer morning   You could have
sworn you remembered it raining   It
had not rained   It had never
poured and here you sat patiently
waiting while attending to the particulars
of a murder although you felt
in the back of your brain
all that stirring thunder that you
realized had never happened   You were
doubtlessly dreaming   You must have been
sleeping   You listened as she explained
exactly how the man was discovered
dead in the forest a few
years ago   His body had been
absent for months   Your hostess it
turns out had reason to suspect
nearly everyone   After all Chadron was
a small town and in a
small town everyone knows just about
everything about everyone else who is
living there—for example they might

understand why a man would most
likely not chain his body to
a tree just to burn to
death   She said that he was
discovered drunk but never drank   He
was found uphill but had trouble
hiking   He was remembered as quiet
and tired and kind and was
lit on fire by either his
own hand or his own friends
or some unknown local adversary   You
heard this story the morning you
awoke in the Olde Main Street
Inn in Nebraska   The prior evening
you'd observed a series of brutal
turquoise clouds bruising the lilac sky
like you could never divine in
your whole life and—*Dear Reader*—
it was still two nights before
those striking Badlands stars were

Acknowledgments

Thank you to the editors of the following journals for publishing poems from this manuscript:

Cant: "Vision #1," "Vision #3"
Driftless Review: "Four Dead Men" (reprint)
Free Verse: "Rumors"
Iowa Review: "Telephone," "Mausoleum"
Inter/rupture: "The Heart"
The New Old Stock: "The Traveler"
notnostrums: "The Haunting"
Poetry Daily: "Telephone" (reprint)
Poetry International: "Olde Main Street Inn"
Thermos: "Badlands," "Four Dead Men"
They Will Sew The Blue Sail (*VOLTA*): "Old Wars"
Verse Wisconsin: "The Motley Cow"
Wintered Chaplet Series: "Telephone," "Telling Jokes," "The Haunting," "Mausoleum"
Women's Quarterly Conversation: "Ghost Town"

Thank you to Mary Biddinger, Amy Freels, and everyone at the University of Akron Press for giving *Twice Told* a second life. Thank you to Heidi Reszies and Nate Slawson for their work on the original version of this book and for continued use of the skull. Thank you to Ossian Foley for his permanent memento mori.

Caryl Pagel holds a BA from the University of Wisconsin-Madison and MFAs from the School of the Art Institute of Chicago and the Iowa Writers' Workshop. She is the author of two collections of poetry, *Twice Told* (University of Akron Press) and *Experiments I Should Like Tried at My Own Death* (Factory Hollow Press). Her poetry and prose have appeared in *AGNI*, *The Collagist*, *Entropy*, *The Iowa Review*, *The Mississippi Review*, and *The Paris Review*, among other journals. Caryl is the cofounder and editor of Rescue Press, a poetry editor at *jubilat*, and the director of the Cleveland State University Poetry Center. She is an assistant professor at Cleveland State University, where she teaches poetry and nonfiction for undergraduates and in the NEOMFA program. She is the recipient of grants and residencies from Cleveland State University, Headlands Center for the Arts, The Hermitage Artist Retreat, and the Ohio Arts Council.